Kindle Ad Campaigns That Work

A Report on 40 Campaigns I Tried.
Some Worked.

By Steven C. Fotheringham

Why You Need This Book

The value of Amazon's Kindle Ad Campaigns is that they target people who are looking for books—better yet, books in your book's category. Michael Alvear, in his book *Make a Killing on Kindle . . . ,* argues that the best way to sell a Kindle book is to do so in the Kindle environment.

The problem with Kindle Ads is you have to pay to see if they work. And they often don't. Four or five loosing campaigns are enough to get us looking elsewhere to market our books. But, I kept trying. I ran 40 different campaigns promoting three fictional books and one biography. Some of them bombed. Some of them promoted my books and actually made a profit.

Due Diligence

I once asked a friend for advice about investing in a piece of property. He came to my office with a book the size of an old family Bible. He said "We have a computer program that asks hundreds of questions about a property we're interested in. It costs us about $20,000 to obtain all the answers. It generates this report. If it concludes that the development is a bad investment, that $20,000 is the best money we could have spent." He called that exercise "due diligence."

Those who are reading this understand "due diligence." If this book helps someone decide not to run a campaign, the price of this book will have been well worth it. That being said, I want this to be real diligence.

In her book *Kindle Ad Campaigns Can Running Ads Through Amazon Marketing Services Help You Sell More Books?*, Barb Asselin took five of her books and ran basically the same campaign on each of them for a couple weeks. She bid about 5 cents per click and got dismal results. She cancelled her campaigns before they cost her anything. The following are her conclusions in part:

Ultimately, I was disappointed in the performance of the ads. Here's what I think I could have done differently:

- I could have run the ads for a longer period of time, but I felt that 2–3 full weeks (including weekdays and weekends) were sufficient to account for any ebbs and flows in customer engagement.

- I could have picked more products to target.

- I could have chosen different books or different niches.

- I could have chosen a higher price per click, however, I used the suggested amount that Amazon gave me.

- I could have let the ads run at the discretion of Amazon, instead of spacing them out equally among the time period, however, I did not want to get stuck with a $500 advertising bill for just 1 or 2 days. I don't think that I could have changed categories, as the categories were very broad and certain books only fit 1 or 2 categories.

- Let the Ads run at Amazon's discretion, and

- Had a fiction book to try it out on.

On the up side, my 5 ad campaigns cost me NOTHING. I still have my $500 that I intended to pay for the ad clicks. So, what's next? I am definitely not giving up on Kindle Ad Campaigns, but I'll have to try something different next time.

With all due respect, that wasn't very diligent.

I was determined to find a campaign that works. I was willing to "get stuck with a $500 advertising bill" if that could teach me anything. I set aside $5,000 for my campaigns. I figured that would promote my books and be adequate tuition to learn the Kindle ad system. But no matter how I tried, I couldn't spend $5,000. Amazon never used all of my budgets for my campaigns. And I kept selling books.

I wanted to know if repeated campaigns would have a cumulative effect. Would sales increase because of repeated exposure? What happens when a person sees my ad a few times? Does that eventually get them to click on my ad? Am I a marketer like Geico, or am I a book seller? Marketing takes time and diligence. That's what I offer in this book.

The reader may want me to cut to the chase—just give a spread sheet showing all my campaigns. But net sales don't tell the whole story. There are things I learned from each campaign. I think those things will spark ideas for marketers. Therefore this book is a journey, my learning curve, if you will, on how I tried to promote my books.

My approach was simple. I described my Kindle Ad Campaign and reported the results. I changed a variable on that campaign and tried again. This is not perfect science. But it gave the answers I was looking for.

About my Book

My biography is called "Wheelz." It is about my son who is likely the most famous wheelchair athlete in the world. He was the first to do a back-flip, a front-flip and a double back-flip in a wheelchair. He has 3 Guinness world records, a couple Nike commercials, he performs with Nitro Circus, and well I'll stop there.

The problem with my book is the cover. Marcelo Sayao, a professional photographer, got a great shot of my son on a huge ramp in Brazil. It showed up in Sports Illustrated. I had to have that picture for the cover. It cost a lot. It's beautiful. But it appeals to the wrong audience. My son's fans (and I assume extreme sports fans in general) are not avid readers. Adults, especially women, like my book. That's great because women read a lot. But there is nothing on my cover that says "Even if you care zero about extreme sports you'll like this story." All of this is to say your results may vary on your book(s). A how to, or a fiction, or a book with a strait-forward cover may do much better.

And yet, an Ad Campaign can help me say "You don't have to be into horse racing to like Laura Hillenbrand's Seabiscuit. You'll enjoy this book."

One advantage of my book is my son has about 200,000 followers on Instagram that he faithfully posts to every day. I figured one shout out from him and the book would jump to page one in its category. I was wrong. We did sell a few books when we launched it. But sales fell to basically nothing after a few months.

Here's how my books sold between August (launch date) through November 2015

Kindle Book	Sold 76 for $3.99 per book	Royalty $2.79 $212.27
Audio Book	Sold 23 for $17.46 per book	Royalty $4.15 $95.45
Paper Back Book	Sold 225 for $13.97 per book	Royalty $3.18 $715.50

The stats (the rankings) on my book are meaningless. In three days I went from 471,672 in Bestseller rank to 139,176 then back up to 459,553. I had no activity (no sales) on my book on those days. I was ranked 876 in Self-help > Motivational books on one day. The next day there was no listing under that category. It will be interesting to see if multiple ad campaigns result in better rankings. But I don't trust them. KDP reports number of copies sold. That is an important measurement. But number of impressions (the number of people that are shown your ad) are what I think would be of most interest to the reader. The campaign that generates a lot of impressions is what we want. The number of books sold will depend if those people are interested in your book or not. And obviously my sales and your sales will be different.

Before my first ad campaign I had 26 reviews—all positive.

Setting up an Ad Campaign Step by Step

First of all, you need to sign up for **Kindle Select** to run a Kindle Ad Campaign. Once you have done that follow these steps.

1. Log on to KDP.Amazon.Com

2. Click on or log into your account. On my heading it says "Steve's Account" I click on that.

3. Sign in

4. Click on "Bookshelf"

5. Click on your book you want to promote.

6. Click on "Promote and advertise"

7. Click on "Create an ad campaign"

8. Click on Product Display Ads (we will look at Sponsored Products later)

9. Click on By Interest or By Product

10. Fill in the blanks (this book will be about how I filled in the blanks for each campaign)

My Kindle Ad Campaigns

Campaign name	Wheelz 1
Book	Wheelz
Ad locations	Detail pages on Amazon.com
Targeting type	Product-based (one book)
Targeted expansion	On
CPC bid	$0.70
Budget	$100
Duration	10/07/2015–01/06/2016
Pacing	Allow Amazon to spread out my campaign smoothly
Kindle book price	$2.99

I bid $0.70 because (according to Amazon) my "actual cost-per-click (CPC) is determined in an auction that takes place with other eligible ads." [I] will be charged $0.01 more than the second-highest bid in the auction for a click, up to [my] maximum CPC bid." $0.70 will pretty much guarantee I'll be the highest bidder.

I targeted my ad "By product." I wanted to be on the first page of "Motivational books." When I searched on "Motivational books" the first book to come up was "How Successful People Think." That book is the only product I added. I tailored my ad to talk about seeing things in an un-habitual way. I assumed that would appeal to people who are interested in how successful people think. I wondered if it matters at all. Of course I would like to attract people to my book. But what if it read "Eat more pork?" Fewer people would click on my ad. But I only pay per click. So it will take longer to use up my $100, but I will get more impressions for no cost.

Results: After two weeks:

Impressions	7201
Clicks	4
CTR	.056% (Click through rate)
Spend	$1.73
ACPC	$0.43 (Average cost per click)
Estimated orders	0
Estimated total sales	$0.00

I lost $1.73 on this campaign.

I was determined to ride this ad out for a month. But there is no benefit in doing that. With the experience I got from other ads (detailed below) I realized the cost per click is too high and the number of impressions are poor. So I cancelled this ad after 15 days.

* * *

Campaign name	Wheelz 2
Book	Wheelz
Ad locations	Detail pages on Amazon.com
Targeting type	Product-based (five books)
Targeted expansion	On
CPC bid	$0.70
Budget	$100.00
Duration	12/08/2015–01/07/2016
Pacing	Allow Amazon to spread out my campaign smoothly
Kindle book price	$2.99

Is it better to have more products? The only difference on my second ad was that I chose 5 of the top books in the category of "Motivational books."

Results after two weeks.

Impressions	14,923
Clicks	6
CTR	.045% (Click through rate)
Spend	$3.09
ACPC	$0.52 (Average cost per click)
Estimated orders	0
Estimated total sales	$0.00

I lost $3.09 on this campaign.

So far it is clear that multiple products (more books selected) yields more impressions (as compared to Wheelz 1, one book selected). I have also learned that the first week of a campaign yields many more impressions than the second week, at least that's true on my first two campaigns. In these campaigns I let "Amazon spread out my campaign smoothly." I also cancelled this ad after 15 days.

* * *

I emailed Amazon and asked if two ads at $0.70 would push my costs per click (CPC) up—if I am bidding against myself. They responded "As all the scheduled campaigns need to get into auction. So in your scenario, you yourself will be your own competitor." Therefore two ads from the same individual, aimed at the same product or same interests, would not be wise. And yet, my CPC was actually $0.52, not $0.70. So it is not clear how they determine the highest bidder.

* * *

Campaign name	**Wheelz 3**
Book	Wheelz
Ad locations	Detail pages on Amazon.com
Targeting type	Product-based (one book)
Targeted expansion	On
CPC bid	$0.70
Budget	$100.00
Duration	12/09/2015–01/08/2016
Pacing	Allow Amazon to spread out my campaign smoothly
Kindle book price	$2.99

Does the wording in an ad matter? This ad targeted only one book like my first ad Wheelz 1. The wording on my first two ads was ""True genius is the ability to see things in an un-habitual way. It is the greatest gift one human being can give another." "William James."" On this ad I changed my my wording to ""When life gives you a wheelchair go find a skate park." Aaron "Wheelz" Fotheringham.""

Results: After two weeks:

Impressions	13,810
Clicks	3
CTR	.022% (Click through rate)
Spend	$1.52
ACPC	$0.51 (Average cost per click)
Estimated orders	0
Estimated total sales	0

I lost $1.52 on this campaign.

On this ad my impressions were more "smooth" on each week. But the second week was still less. I received the following from Amazon Marketing Services. "Thank you for using Amazon Marketing Services. Your campaign, "Wheelz 3" was stopped due to low relevance." My first ad Wheelz 1 had less impressions but 4 clicks (one more click than Wheelz 3), so it wasn't cancelled. I don't think there is enough data to determine if ad wording made any difference.

* * *

Amazon will not approve ads that say such things as "Free," "$0.99," "$2.99" in your wording. You also cannot quote reader reviews.

* * *

Campagin name	**Wheelz 4**
Book	Wheelz
Ad locations	Detail pages on Amazon.com
Targeting type	Interest-based
Targeted Interests	Biographies & Memoirs: Leaders & Notable People, Memoirs, Sports
CPC bid	$0.05
Budget	$100.00
Duration	12/10/2015–01/09/2016
Pacing	Allow Amazon to spread out my campaign smoothly
Kindle book price	$2.99

What if we bid only $0.05? This campaign is interest-based. I also changed my ad wording to read ""Some people see a wheelchair as constraining. I see it as an extreme sport." Aaron "Wheelz" Fotheringham.""

Results: After 3 weeks

Impressions	36,279
Clicks	248
CTR	.0684% (Click through rate)
Spend	$10.80
ACPC	$0.40 (Average cost per click)
Estimated orders	6
Estimated total sales	$12.24 (My report says $20.94 but that's total gross sales. My net royalty at $2.04 per book is $12.24).

I made $1.44 on this ad. Whoo haa! I'm making money.

I think that shows I found good wording for my ad. Interest based targeting with multiple interests seems to be better than targeting one book. $0.05 CPC bid only cost $0.04 per click.

Had I maintained my $0.70 ad and garnered 248 clicks it would have cost me around $124.00 (at about $0.50 actual CPC). Such high bidding is not sustainable. For that matter if I bid Amazon's recommended $0.30 to $0.38 those 248 clicks would have cost me $74.00 to $94.00 respectively. I should try a $.30 CPC ad to see what they're thinking, but so far it makes no sense. Bidding $0.05 CPC with a $100.00 budget is pretty good.

Campaign name	**Wheelz 5**
Book	Wheelz
Ad locations	Detail pages on Amazon.com
Targeting type	Interest-based
Targeted Interests	Biographies & Memoirs: Leaders & Notable People, Memoirs, Sports
CPC bid	$0.05
Budget	$500.00
Duration	12/10/2015–01/09/2016
Pacing	Allow Amazon to spread out my campaign smoothly
Kindle book price	$2.99

What if our budget was $500.00? That is the only difference from Wheelz 4?

Results: after a month

Impressions	50,460
Clicks	308
CTR	.061% (Click through rate)

Spend	$12.50
ACPC	$0.04 (Average cost per click)
Estimated orders	7
Estimated total sales	$14.28

I made $1.78 on this campaign.

Ad budget amount seems to be more important than an extremely high bid (such as my $0.70 bid). $0.05 bids are good. $500 budget is really good. My CTR is good. I will stay with my ad wording for a while.

* * *

Campaign name	**Wheelz 6**
Book	Wheelz
Ad locations	Detail pages on Amazon.com
Targeting types	Interest-based
Targeted Interests	Biographies & Memoirs: Leaders & Notable People, Memoirs, Sports
CPC bid	$0.05
Budget	$500.00

Duration	12/10/2015–01/09/2016
Pacing	Allow Amazon to spread out my campaign
Kindle book price	$2.99

This campaign is different from Wheelz 5 only in the pacing option is "Deliver my campaign as quickly as possible."

Results: After one month

Impressions	51,454
Clicks	328
CTR	.0637% (Click through rate)
Spend	$13.05
ACPC	$0.04 (Average cost per click)
Estimated orders	6
Estimated total sales	$12.24

I lost $0.81 on this campaign

The impressions on Wheelz 6 are more than Wheelz 5, but not by much. But the first week Wheelz 6 impressions were way ahead of Wheelz 5 (like 2,000 more). After about 12 days the smooth delivery campaign caught up. If you wanted to run a campaign for just a week then cancel it, "as quickly as possible" would it bring more impressions?

It may seem like making so little and actually loosing a little on these campaigns means Kindle ads are not worth the time or effort. On the contrary people are reading my book. That in itself is a good thing. The following blog post is helpful. Gerald Bond wrote,

> For a majority of people, if it requires any effort at all, even clicking a link and then downloading etc, well, so many people have better things to do.

> So what is the answer? Marketing marketing marketing, then you can raise your head above the average sea level just a bit. Then, if you are lucky, enough people will see your head bobbing on the water.

So I don't consider that -$0.81 as a loss. My borrowed reads (KENP explained later) most likely will make up for that. The question I had before I started any of these ad campaigns was can they work? I Googled that question and the overall consensus was "No." But then I read this blog.

A Different Point Of View Said On 28-08-2015, Author unknown.

> I've been writing for about 20 years. Everybody writes for different reasons. One of course is money; early on, I was in that group: I thought writing was going to make me rich or something. Now, I just write because I write, mainly. That being said, I don't do anything else but write, read, edit, just surf the net reading about

publishing and everything; I'm addicted to the whole thing to be honest. Further, I'm one of these writers who lives at the top of the Ivory Tower. It's just me, what I think is my genius, and lots of free hours to spend as I want . . . mainly on the things I mentioned above: writing, editing, reading, surfing the net about publishing. Personally, I think I have more knowledge than 99% percent of the people in publishing out there. That being said, I really don't give out tricks of the trade . . . things that I've picked up over the years. But sometimes I do. I read over all the comments above. Everybody's wrong. Not only are you wrong, but you're actually on the right path, you just don't know it. First, selling books is a bitch. Everybody knows that. That being said, not to digress anymore, I think if the authors who posted above remember this little fact that slips our minds sometimes when it comes to selling books, you'd see how using Amazon's advertising platform above, even with 0 clicks, is still very beneficial to you, and not only that, but it's even great that you have all those free impressions without being charged! (And no, I don't work for Amazon.)

Years ago, very early on, when I got the itch to write, when I thought I was going to become the richest writer in America with the largest house in Palm Beach, throwing the most gigantic parties the universe has ever seen, I spent countless hours at the library. I read all types of books dealing with publishing. I figured at one point, if I was in college, all these books I read, I'd probably have two phds. Anyhow. Part of the 3-headed monster, Cerberus, marketing and advertising and pr . . . all books on these three subjects, all kind of related, said the same thing when it comes to selling anything. If you remember this lesson, you won't doubt yourself as much, and you won't think you efforts are in vain.

I'm going on the basis that all writers who posted above are unknowns. All the books said, when it comes to selling anything, when you're an unknown–trying to make a cold sale, it's virtually impossible. For a potential reader to buy a book from you, that potential reader, on average, has to have heard of your name or your product, and in this case, your book, about seven times beforehand.

Ask yourself, say you had 1,000 impressions using Amazon's platform above, how many of those people actually saw the impression? But better yet, of the people who saw your impression–your name and book, how many of those people had seen your name or book's name before? I'd have to guess none.

You as a writer–if you're an unknown, look at it this way, honestly, from what I've read in the books, tried and true, you really have to touch a potential reader–a cold sale, seven times.

A side note, to touch a potential reader 7 times–to make them aware of your book–to have the thought of you or your book lingering in their mind, personally, I believe you have to have your book on no less than 50 platforms or plugged into 50 different outlets.

Just think about it, if you only have 7 outlets, and you're an unknown, what are the chances that a potential reader–a cold sale, is gonna tap into all 7 of those outlets? I'd say none. There's no chance that potential reader is gonna cross paths with the 7 or so outlets or platforms you have set up. No way.

All the above being said, all the writers who used Amazon's advertising platform above, who think it was useless, I'd say this. Say for example, you got 0 clicks and 1,000 impressions. I don't know how many readers actually saw those impressions. That being said, let's say 500 saw them. So what you did is this (and for free may I add), you've touched those 500 readers one time each; they either know your name or your book's name now. Next time they come across your name or book's name, they won't be unfamiliar with you: it won't be a cold sale. It'll now be a lukewarm sale . . . potential sale.

I think everybody above is on the right path. They just don't know it. If you can get free impressions from Amazon, take'em!

Also, think about your own experience. Don't you every now and then again see an ad for a book. Don't think much of it, because you've never heard of it. But when you see it again, it clicks something in your mind. I don't know what it is, but it does. Anyhow

So I do not consider a $0.81 negative as a loss.

* * *

The preview of my ads shows my cover and the ad text, but no heading. When my ad was approved I got an email giving me a link to my "ad dashboard." That sends me to my "Advertising Campaigns." I bookmarked that link for future reports.

When I click on "Wheez 6" under "Campaign Name" it gives the details of my campaign. At the bottom of the page it offers a link that says "Preview ad." That link shows my ad in different sizes. As I look at each size I realize my heading will be displayed in some of my ads. It is a goofy heading. It says "Some people see a wheelchair as constraining." I did that because I didn't know my heading shows. I will try to improve my headings.

The bottom line is, notwithstanding my poor heading, my clicks and my CTR (Click Through Rate) is much higher with this ad wording.

* * *

Campaign name	**Wheelz 7**
Book	Wheelz
Ad locations	Detail pages on Amazon.com
Targeting type	Interest-based
Targeted Interests	Biographies & Memoirs: Leaders & Notable People, Memoirs, Sports
CPC bid	$0.02
Budget	$500.00
Duration	12/10/2015–01/09/2016
Pacing	Deliver my campaign as quickly as possible
Kindle book price	$2.99

Two changes on this campaign. My heading "Be inspired." And $0.02 CPC bid.

Results: After 9 days:

Impressions	38
Clicks	0
CTR	.0% (Click through rate)

Spend	$0.00
ACPC	$0.00 (Average cost per click)
Estimated orders	0
Estimated total sales	$0.00

Conclusion: $.02 CPC is a waste of time. I will change it to $0.04.

Campaign name	**Wheelz 8**
Book	Wheelz
Ad locations	Detail pages on Amazon.com
Targeting type	Interest-based
Targeted Interests	Biographies & Memoirs: Leaders & Notable People, Memoirs, Sports
CPC bid	$0.04
Budget	$500.00
Duration	12/10/2015–01/09/2016
Pacing	Deliver my campaign as quickly as possible
Kindle book price	$2.99

Results: After 11 days:

Impressions	1,226
Clicks	0
CTR	.0%
Spend	$0.00
ACPC	$0.00 (Average cost per click)
Estimated orders	0
Estimated total sales	0

Conclusion: After eleven days $0.04 did no good. I will close this campaign.

* * *

Campaign name	**Wheelz 9**
Book	Wheelz
Ad locations	Detail pages on Amazon.com
Targeting type	Product-based
Targeted Interests	19 targeted products (19 top

selling books) inspiration and motivation

CPC bid	$0.02
Budget	$500.00
Duration	12/10/2015–01/09/2016
Pacing	Deliver my campaign as quickly as possible
Kindle book price	$2.99

This time I targeted a lot of books.

Results: After 7 days:

Impressions	437
Clicks	0
CTR	.0% (Click through rate)
Spend	$0.00
ACPC	$0.00 (Average cost per click)
Estimated orders	0
Estimated total sales	0

Conclusion: $0.02 is a waste of time. But multiple products (19 books) did bring a lot of impressions compared to my other $0.02 campaigns.

Campaign name	Wheelz 10
Book	Wheelz
Ad locations	Detail pages on Amazon.com
Targeting type	Product-based
Targeted Interests	19 targeted products (19 top selling books) inspiration and motivation
CPC bid	$0.04
Budget	$500.00
Duration	12/10/2015–01/09/2016
Pacing	Deliver my campaign as quickly as possible
Kindle book price	$2.99

Results: After 20 days:

Impressions	300
Clicks	0
CTR	.0% (Click through rate)
Spend	$0.00
ACPC	$0.00 (Average cost per click)
Estimated orders	0
Estimated total sales	0

Conclusion: Bidding anything between $0.01 to $0.04 is not worth the time it takes to set up the campaign. I will terminate this campaign also.

* * *

Campaign name	**Wheelz 11**
Book	Wheelz
Ad locations	Detail pages on Amazon.com
Targeting type	Interest-based
Targeted Interests	23 interests targeted
CPC bid	$0.02

Budget	$500.00
Duration	12/10/2015–01/09/2016
Pacing	Deliver my campaign as quickly as possible
Kindle book price	$2.99

Only difference is multiple interests targeted instead of multiple products.

Results: after 9 days:

Impressions	17
Clicks	0
CTR	.0% (Click through rate)
Spend	$0.00
ACPC	$0.00 (Average cost per click)
Estimated orders	0
Estimated total sales	$0.00

Again bidding $0.02 is worthless regardless of how many interests were targeted.

Campaign name	**Wheelz 12**
Book	Wheelz
Ad locations	Detail pages on Amazon.com
Targeting type	Interest-based
Targeted Interests	23 interests targeted
CPC bid	$0.04
Budget	$1,000.00
Duration	12/10/2015–01/09/2016
Pacing	Deliver my campaign as quickly as possible
Kindle book price	$2.99

Results: After 17 days:

Impressions	141
Clicks	0
CTR	.0% (Click through rate)
Spend	$0.00
ACPC	$0.00 (Average cost per click)
Estimated orders	0

Estimated total sales $0.00

Conclusion: After 17 days I raised the bid to $0.04. I only got 141 impressions. The $1,000 didn't help the campaign. The bottom line is $0.04 CPC bids are no good. Multiple interests did better than a few interests targeted.

* * *

Wheelz 4, 5 and 6 at $0.05, $500 budget so far have been my best ads. They each targeted 3 interests. Wheelz 6, 7 and 8 suggest they would have done even better if I targeted products (a good number of books). By targeting multiple books I think I can run multiple ads without bidding against myself. I'll choose different books for each ad.

After a few weeks I noticed my three $0.05 ads at $500 resulted in an average of about one book sold a day. I want to sell 10 books a day. Multiple ad campaigns can help me do that if I can keep from bidding against myself.

* * *

Campaign name	Wheelz 13
Book	Wheelz
Ad locations	Detail pages on Amazon.com
Targeting type	Product-based

Targeted products	40 products targeted
CPC bid	$0.05
Budget	$500.00
Duration	12/28/2015–01/04/2016
Pacing	Deliver my campaign as quickly as possible
Kindle book price	$2.99

My two $0.05 @ $500 campaigns (Wheelz 5 and 6) stalled at about 50,000 impressions after about two weeks. I therefore wanted to see what a one week campaign would do. I set the duration for one week. I could have set it for a month and then cancelled it in a week. But I wanted to see if setting a shorter duration made any difference.

For my targeted products I merely searched for products on the word "success." I added the top 40 books. It was pretty easy. I changed my heading to "It's always hardest right before you succeed"

Results: After 7 days:

Impressions	264
Clicks	0
CTR	.0% (Click through rate)
Spend	$0.00

ACPC	$0.00 (Average cost per click)
Estimated orders	0
Estimated total sales	0

After a week I only had 264 impressions. Wheelz 5 and 6 were set for a month duration. By the first week they had about 25,000 impressions. Setting a campaign for a shorter duration doesn't seem to help.

* * *

After a month my sales are about 50 clicks for one sale. That cost me $2.00 on my $0.05 ads (aCPC being $0.04 aCPC) That $2.00 cost me to get $2.04. So I'm just about breaking even. If I charged $0.99 I would have to sell 7.5 books to break even with my $2.99 charge. I need to try that. I also need to try $3.99. Therefore I will try $0.99.

7 simultaneous $0.99 Wheelz Campaigns

I was selling an average of one book a day with my three $0.05 campaigns. Seven $0.05 campaigns hopefully will raise that average. The only difference in the campaigns is the targeted products or interests and on one ad I'm bidding $0.06 CPC. My Kindle book price is

$.99 for each campaign.

Campaign name	Wheelz 14
Book	Wheelz
Ad locations	Detail pages on Amazon.com
Targeting type	Product-based
Targeted products	10 products targeted (In "Success Books" category)
CPC bid	$0.05
Budget	$500.00
Duration	01/05/2016–02/04/2016
Pacing	Deliver my campaign as quickly

	as possible
Kindle book price	$0.99

This time I chose the top ten books that had numerous reviews.

Results after 13 days

Impressions	125
Clicks	0
CTR	.0% (Click through rate)
Spend	$0.00
ACPC	$0.00 (Average cost per click)
Estimated orders	0
Estimated total sales	$0.00

Of my 7 simultaneous campaigns only 2 did anything. It is as if Amazon limits how many impressions a book can get regardless of number of campaigns. I can test this by running this campaign all on its own.

Campaign name	**Wheelz 15**
Book	Wheelz
Ad locations	Detail pages on Amazon.com
Targeting type	Product-based
Targeted products	10 products targeted (in "Inspirational Books" category)
CPC bid	$0.05
Budget	$500.00
Duration	01/05/2016–02/04/2016
Pacing	Deliver my campaign as quickly as possible
Kindle book price	$0.99

The only difference is Targeted Products.

Results after 13 days

Impressions	310
Clicks	0
CTR	.0% (Click through rate)
Spend	$0.00

ACPC	$0.00 (Average cost per click)
Estimated orders	0
Estimated total sales	$0.00

Like Wheelz 14 this was a nothing campaign.

Campaign name	**Wheelz 16**
Book	Wheelz
Ad locations	Detail pages on Amazon.com
Targeting type	Product-based
Targeted products	10 products (from top 100 Kindle bookstore best sellers)
CPC bid	$0.05
Budget	$500.00
Duration	01/05/2016–02/04/2016
Pacing	Deliver my campaign as quickly as possible
Kindle book price	$0.99

Heading: "Be Inspired."

The only difference is Targeted Products

Results after 13 days

Impressions	619
Clicks	1
CTR	.162% (Click through rate)
Spend	$0.05
ACPC	$0.05 (Average cost per click)
Estimated orders	0
Estimated total sales	0

Like Wheelz 14 and 15, this was a nothing campaign

Campaign name	**Wheelz 17**
Book	Wheelz
Ad locations	Detail pages on Amazon.com
Targeting type	Product-based
Targeted products	10 products targeted (in

	"Biography Books" category)
CPC bid	$0.05
Budget	$500.00
Duration	01/05/2016–01/04/2016
Pacing	Deliver my campaign as quickly as possible
Kindle book price	$0.99

The only difference is Targeted Products

Results after 13 days

Impressions	1,432
Clicks	1
CTR	.07% (Click through rate)
Spend	$0.05
ACPC	$0.05 (Average cost per click)
Estimated orders	0
Estimated total sales	$0.00

Also a loser campaign

Campaign name	Wheelz 18
Book	Wheelz
Ad locations	Detail pages on Amazon.com
Targeting type	Interest-based
Targeted Interests	7 interests targeted (all under Biographies)
CPC bid	$0.06
Budget	$500.00
Duration	01/05/2016–02/04/2016
Pacing	Deliver my campaign as quickly as possible
Kindle book price	$0.99

The differences are $0.06 CPC bid and Interests Targeted.

Results after 13 days

Impressions	93
Clicks	0
CTR	.0% (Click through rate)
Spend	$0.00

ACPC	$0.00 (Average cost per click)
Estimated orders	0
Estimated total sales	$0.00

Wheelz 4, 5 and 6 Targeted Biographies. They got between 35,000 and 50,000 impressions. They all had a bid of $0.05 CPC. They also all died half way through my campaigns at about 50,000 impressions. They were, in my opinion, successful campaigns. When I tried to repeat the campaign (same interests targeted), and even bidding $0.06 CPC, my impressions were pathetic. I either used up all the impressions I can get in that category or my multiple campaigns are getting in the way.

Campaign name	**Wheelz 19**
Book	Wheelz
Ad locations	Detail pages on Amazon.com
Targeting type	Interest-based
Targeted Interests	7 Interests targeted (under "Health, Fitness, and Dieting)
CPC bid	$0.05
Budget	$500.00

Duration	01/05/2016–01/04/2016
Pacing	Deliver my campaign as quickly as possible
Kindle book price	$0.99

Heading: "Be Inspired"

The difference is Interests Targeted

Results after 13 days

Impressions	53.078
Clicks	333
CTR	.627%
Spend	$13.65
ACPC	$0.04 (Average cost per click)
Estimated orders	12
Estimated total sales	$11.88

12 X $0.35 Royalty = $4.20 Royalty $4.20 - $13.65 = -$9.45 lost on this campaign. But I sold 12 books.

Campaign name	**Wheelz 20**
Book	Wheelz
Ad locations	Detail pages on Amazon.com
Targeting type	Interest-based
Targeted Interests	8 Interest targeted (under "Romance")
CPC bid	$0.05
Budget	$500.00
Duration	01/05/2016–02/04/2016
Pacing	Deliver my campaign as quickly as possible
Kindle book price	$3.99

The difference is Interests Targeted and book price is $3.99.

Results after 13 days

Impressions	24,732
Clicks	159
CTR	.643% (Click through rate)
Spend	$6.30

ACPC	$0.04 (Average cost per click)
Estimated orders	1
Estimated total sales	$3.99

1 book for $2.40 (commission on $3.99 book) = $2.40 - $6.30 (spent on clicks) = -$3.90 lost on campaign.

I lost $3.90 on this campaign. But notice my targeted audience was under "Romance." My impressions were high and my click through rate was as good as if my target audience was "Motivational Biographies."

Book pricing results

$0.99 = 1 book sold for every 27.75 clicks. Royalty for $0.99 is $0.35. 27.75 clicks at $0.04 per click (although my bid was $0.05) = $1.11. So I lost $0.76 for every book I sold.

$2.99 = 1 book sold for every 50 clicks. Royalty for $2.99 is $2.04. 50 clicks for $0.04 per click (although I bid $0.05) = $2.00. So I gained $0.04 for every book I sold.

$3.99 = 1 book sold for every 159 clicks. Royalty for $3.99 is $2.40. 159 clicks for $0.04 = $6.36. So I lost $3.96 for every book I sold.

$0.99 yields a lot of sales per click. But each sale cost me about $0.76 on clicks. Before my Kindle Ad Campaigns I paid an author advertising site $25.00 to advertise my book selling at $0.99. I sold 15 books on that site. Kindle Ads costing $1.11 per book would have sold 22.5 books for $25.00.

I was willing to lose on each book sale if it moved up my book's ranking. But Amazon's ranking for Wheelz was like a roller-coaster. It shot down, then up, then down again, regardless of sales. I think when you get on top of the ranking it means something. The bottom line is I couldn't tell if $0.99 did my book any good in ranking.

$3.99 is a money loser.

But 12 people (from my $0.99 per book ad) reading my book is important to me. I think they will like my book and tell others about it. The following is an article from an author group in Goodreads.

B.B. Wynter
Mod

> I think a lot of it has to do with that now there is the internet, people are being flooded with so much information daily. It is constant. There are all kinds of things to read. There are 2 million ebooks on Amazon, all wanting to be the top, to have a career like J.K. Rowling has.
>
> I do believe that the more persistent you are, the more you push, the more it will work. People want to feel engaged and personal too. A good friend of mine who is a New York businessman, once taught me that if you stand on the street and talk to people, you have more luck selling your craft, because they feel a part of what you have created . . . there is something about meeting a real life author.

It can take a lifetime for a person's work to be acknowledged. Even though we are bombarded with successful celebrities and how rich and important they are, art is a journey that requires your commitment and unwavering passion for decades. You have to keep showing people and convince them that they will feel moved by your creations, and entice them into the possibility.

It helps to connect with those who are passionate in the same genres that you are too, that is a journey as well.

But I think that if you don't see this as a goal to be successful with fame and money, and see it as a journey of art instead, and connecting with others as an author and artist, it will feel less defeating and more elevating and inspiring. Essentially, you are an entertainer, a muse, channeling fantasies and emotions, experiences and memories for others.

That being said I was able to sell about a book a day at $2.99 per book without losing money. I have read that $2.99 is the optimum Kindle Book price. My experience seems to bear that out. And $0.05 seems to be a smart bid price.

On January 18th, 2016 I stopped my 7 simultaneous ads and put my price back to $2.99. I wanted to try Wheelz 14 all on its own. After 13 days (running simultaneously) it had only 125 impressions. The duplicate campaign will be called Wheelz 21. The only differences will be the price of my book and it will not run with other ads. I will run it for two weeks and see if it beats 125 impressions. I will choose the same 10 books under "Targeted products."

Campaign name	Wheelz 21
Book	Wheelz
Ad locations	Detail pages on Amazon.com
Targeting type	Product-based
Targeted products	10 products targeted (In "Success Books" category)
CPC bid	$0.05
Budget	$500.00
Duration	01/18/2016–02/17/2016
Pacing	Deliver my campaign as quickly as possible
Kindle book price	$2.99

Under "How do I re-run a campaign?" we find,

"If your campaign is running, you can extend the end date and increase the budget by editing the existing campaign. If your campaign has ended, you will need to create a new campaign." I just ended all my campaigns and duplicated Wheelz 14. As a simultaneous add it got only 126 impressions. I wanted to see if the same ad would do well on its own.

Results after 20 days

Impressions	206
Clicks	1
CTR	.485% (Click through rate)
Spend	$0.04
ACPC	$0.04 (Average cost per click)
Estimated orders	0
Estimated total sales	$0.00

Wheelz 21 on its own did no better than Wheelz 14 (that was advertising with 6 other campaigns). Both were nothing campaigns. I sold no books off that campaign. The one person that clicked didn't buy. And yet my KDP reports shows I sold 5 books during the last 20 days. I believe that is momentum off my previous campaigns.

To date (about two months of campaigns) I have spent $61.61. So far I have sold 49 books—10 at $0.99 = $3.50 Royalty, 1 at $3.99 = $2.74 Royalty, 38 at $2.99 = $77.52, for a total of $83.76. My profit is $22.15. That's a net profit of $11.07 per month.

I spent about $22,000 to produce my book, not to mention 5 years in writing it. At a net profit of $11.07 per month I should recoup my investment in about 165 years. However 49 people are reading my book since I started my Kindle campaigns. And I got one review. I believe my book helps people. I would pay money to do that. Right now it cost me $449 per book to inspire someone. In a year of selling 25 books a month I will have sold 300 books. Then each book would have cost me $73 to make a difference in a person's life. If I could help someone with a serious challenge (and we all have serious challenges) get a new view on life for $73.00, I would do that every day of the week. And the more I sell, the more that cost comes down. I also love reading reviews. Don't get me wrong. I wrote the book to make money. Maybe with consistent marketing I will. Until then I'll be happy with every book sale and any reviews.

The table shows campaigns that got a lot of impressions.

Wheelz	Impressions	Clicks	Orders	Spend	Sales	ACoS
#4	36,673	249	7	$10.80	$21.93	49.25%
#5	50,462	308	7	$12.50	$22.93	54.51%
#6	51,464	328	6	$13.05	$17.94	72.74%
#19	53,089	334	12	$13.65	$11.88	114.9%
#20	22,547	167	1	$6.65	$3.99	166.6%

ACoS is Average Cost of Sales. Anything under 100% means we make money. For example on Wheelz 4 Sales were $21.93 and I spent $10.80. My ACoS was 49.25% meaning it cost about half of the proceeds of a book to sell a book. Wheelz 20 at $0.99 per book cost the price of a book plus half as much more ($0.66 to be exact) to sell a book.

So far out of 21 campaigns, Wheelz 19 was the best, basing it solely on impressions. That is fascinating because my targeted interests were categories under "Health, Fitness & Dieting." Wheelz 20's targeted interests under the category of "Romance." Its impressions were respectable. When targeting products like various books my impressions were low.

If I try to duplicate Wheelz 19 I doubt it will do much. Campaigns slow down. And stopping a campaign then restarting it, at least on my book, doesn't seem to help. So I need to add something to the mix. I will discontinue Wheelz 21 and run a campaign like Wheelz 19 except I will bid $0.10 per click instead of $0.05. I will call it Wheelz 22. It will be my best campaign ever.

Campaign name	**Wheelz 22**
Book	Wheelz
Ad locations	Detail pages on Amazon.com
Targeting type	Product-based

Targeted Interests	Every sub category under "Health, Fitness & Dieting"
CPC bid	$0.10
Budget	$500.00
Duration	02/06/2016–03/07/2016
Pacing	Deliver my campaign as quickly as possible
Kindle book price	$2.99

Results: After 28 days

Impressions	205,099
Clicks	1,168
CTR	.567% (Click through rate)
Spend	$100.26
ACPC	$0.9 (Average cost per click)
Estimated orders	27
Estimated total sales	$80.73
Estimated gain or loss	-$19.53
ACoS	124.42%

While I was recording the results I got 8 clicks and 1 sale in those few minutes. I would rather at least break even on my campaigns. So I will cancel this ad.

* * *

On our fiction books (which is addressed in the next section) we have a successful campaign (a lot of impressions) under the targeted interests of **Romance** and **Teen and Young Adult**. That has nothing to do with my book. But I want to see if I can get a lot of impressions targeting the same interests.

Campaign name	**Wheelz 23**
Book	Wheelz
Ad locations	Detail pages on Amazon.com
Targeting type	Product-based
Targeted Interests	Romance, Historical Romance, Teen and Young Adult, Historical Fiction, Romance
CPC bid	$0.05
Budget	$500.00
Duration	02/19/2016–03/21/2016

Pacing	Deliver my campaign as quickly as possible
Kindle book price	$2.99

After a week I only have 55 impressions for the Wheelz 23 campaign. Some campaigns take a while to get off the ground so I won't make any conclusions. I wonder if running Wheelz 22 and Wheelz 23 at the same time makes any difference. Wheelz 22 is killing me financially and it may be hurting Wheelz 23. But I will ride it out for another week to see what happens.

After 7 days I had 55 impressions. That's an average of 8 impressions a day.

After 10 days I had 5,386 impressions. That's an average of 538 impressions a day.

I'm picking up steam.

I'm going to report the results of this campaign after 15 days because I ended Wheelz 22. I have reason to believe that simultaneous ads, regardless of having separate categories, hinder each other. But, this is just a guess.

Results: After 15 days.

Impressions	51,506
Clicks	268
CTR	.52% (Click through rate)

Spend	$12.50
ACPC	$0.05 (Average cost per click)
Estimated orders	5
Estimated total sales	$14.95
Estimated gain or loss	$2.45
ACoS	83.61%

This ad fizzled in the end. I'm going to cancel it. It was not helped by discontinuing Wheelz 22.

In Steve Scott's book, *Is $.99 The New Free*, he writes about "Discoverability."

> The interesting thing about Amazon is that success breeds success. What this platform provides is *discoverability*. When a book starts to sell well it gets extra exposure that leads to even more sales. The lesson here is that when you generate the first batch of sales on your own, Amazon will market your book in a variety of places."

Amazon has: Customers Also Bought, Search Engine Results, Category Charts, Special Lists, Kindle Owner' Lending Library, Customized Recommendations, that all promote discoverability.

Before my ads, there was basically no reads in Kindle's borrow program called Kindle Edition Normalized Pages (KENP). Since my ads my KENP reads have been shooting up. One day 600, the next 200, the next 500, the next 300. In my Kindle reports they have a link to "Prior Month's Royalties." In December I made $18.04 on the KENP program. For January I made $16.75 on the KENP program.

People are reading my book. Steve Scott also makes the simple, but crucial, point that **Sales + Borrows = Future Sales.**

Fiction

I thought it would be helpful if we tried ad campaigns on some fictional books. My editor Shaunna Sanders, self-published 2 books, *Good Morning Glory* and *Firebird*. I don't read fiction. But because she helped me with my book I read Firebird.. Frankly I was impressed. She is a great writer. I asked her to let me run her campaigns so we could see how fictional books from an unknown author sell.

Firebird

2 Five Stars reviews

Headline: A wild blend of steampunk and urban fantasy.

Ad text: Lainey has spent her whole life avoiding fairies. But when her new boyfriend disappears, her gift of sight may be the only thing that can save him

* * *

Campaign name	Firebird 1
Book	Firebird
Ad locations	Detail pages on Amazon.com
Targeting type	Interest-based

Targeted Interests	5 Interests selected: Action and adventure, fiction, fantasy, myths and legends, under teen and young adult-science fiction and fantasy
CPC bid	$0.02
Budget	$500.00
Duration	12/17/2015–01/16/2016
Pacing	Deliver my campaign as quickly
Kindle book price	$2.99

* * *

Results: After one week

Impressions	2
Clicks	0
CTR	.0% (Click through rate)
Spend	$0.00
ACPC	$0.00 (Average cost per click)
Estimated orders	0
Estimated total sales	$0.00

After a week we had only two impressions. So I changed the bid to $0.06 CPC.

Campaign name	**Firebird 2**
Book	Firebird
Ad locations	Detail pages on Amazon.com
Targeting type	Interest-based
Targeted Interests	5 Interests science targeted
CPC bid	$0.06
Budget	$500.00
Duration	12/28/2015–01/27/2016
Pacing	Deliver my campaign as quickly as possible
Kindle book price	$2.99

Results: After 4 days:

Impressions	2
Clicks	0
CTR	.0% (Click through rate)

Spend	$0.00
ACPC	$0.00 (Average cost per click)
Estimated orders	0
Estimated total sales	$0.00

After four days at $0.06 we only got 2 impressions. It seems like upgrading a bid amount doesn't do much. $0.06 at $500.00 should have gotten a lot more impressions. I will cancel Firebird 2 and try Firebird 3 at $0.05 per click for a week or two.

* * *

Campaign name	**Firebird 3**
Book	Firebird
Ad locations	Detail pages on Amazon.com
Targeting type	Interest-based
Targeted Interests	5 Interests selected
CPC bid	$0.05
Budget	$500.00
Duration	12/28/2015–01/27/2016
Pacing	Deliver my campaign as quickly

	as possible
Kindle book price	$2.99

Results: After 21 days

Impressions	410,047
Clicks	3,346
CTR	.816% (Click through rate)
Spend	$125.57
ACPC	$0.04 (Average cost per click)
Estimated orders	70
Estimated total sales	$211.42
Estimated gain or loss	$17.23 Gain ($2.04 x 70 = $142.80) ($142.80 - $125.57 = $17.23)
ACoS	59.42%

One book selling for every 47.8 clicks is good. Two amazing things about this campaign, the aCPC's (Average Cost Per Clicks) are averaging $0.04. And 26 orders in the first week shot Firebird to #1 Best Seller in its category.

January 6, 2016, Shaunna's book showed up on page five when searching on "steampunk" in the Kindle store. It shows up on page two when searching on "Children's Steampunk." She is only two books away from being on page one. She is tapping into Amazon's "discoverability" marketing and it cost her nothing.

Jan 7, 2016 Firebird is now on page one. It is #11 when searching "Children's Steampunk." Firebird is #57 of 6,322 and on page four when searching on "Steampunk."

Good Morning Glory (Shaunna's first book) shows up under "Customers who bought this item also bought."

But both Good Morning Glory and Firebird have slowed on number of impressions. I think we need to end the campaigns and then start them again. And Shaunna wants to change the wording on her headings and change the wording in her ads.

Campaign name	Firebird 4
Book	Firebird
Ad locations	Detail pages on Amazon.com
Targeting type	Interest-based
Targeted products	5 Interests selected
CPC bid	$0.05
Budget	$500.00

Duration	01/18/2016–02/17/2016
Pacing	Deliver my campaign as quickly as possible
Kindle book price	$2.99

Headline: "How far would you go to keep a secret?"

Ad Text: "Lainey's always kept to herself. But when Sebastian disappears and her father's framed for his murder, it's time to stop keeping secrets."

Results: After 20 days

Impressions	189
Clicks	1
CTR	.529% (Click through rate)
Spend	$
ACPC	$0.02 (Average cost per click)
Estimated orders	0
Estimated total sales	0
OCoS	0

Steven C. Fotheringham

Firebird 3 had 410,000 impressions in the same amount of time. Firebird 4 only has 189 impressions. We might think that running an identical campaign a second time doesn't work. But we will see that her other book Morning Glory did great with the same campaigns running back to back. I am going to stop Firebird 4 and try $0.06 bid on clicks and change the interests targeted.

Firebird 4 sold no books. And yet Shaunna sold 9 Firebird books during that 20 days (as reported on her KDP report). It appears she's benefiting from the momentum of her previous campaigns.

Campaign name	Firebird 5
Book	Firebird
Ad locations	Detail pages on Amazon.com
Targeting type	Interest-based
Targeted products	11 Interests selected under "Health and Fitness"
CPC bid	$0.06
Budget	$500.00
Duration	02/06/2016–03/07/2016
Pacing	Deliver my campaign as quickly as possible
Kindle book price	$2.99

Results after 28 days

Impressions	36,039
Clicks	209
CTR	.58% (Click through rate)
Spend	$11.82
ACPC	$0.06 (Average cost per click)
Estimated orders	3
Estimated total sales	$8.97
OCoS	113.77%

The bottom line is it cost Shaunna $2.85 to sell 3 books (about $0.95 per book). We're not going to bid $0.06 per click anymore. I'm going to cancel this ad to see if it helps Firebird 7 by not having an ad running at the same time.

Campaign name	**Firebird 6**
Book	Firebird
Ad locations	Detail pages on Amazon.com
Targeting type	Interest-based

Targeted products	10 Interests selected
CPC bid	$0.10
Budget	$1,000.00
Duration	02/13/2016–03/14/2016
Pacing	Deliver my campaign as quickly as possible
Kindle book price	$2.99

This campaign should not compete with Firebird 5 because different interests are targeted. I am bidding $0.10 per click. My Budget is $1,000. It could just as easily be $25,000. It doesn't seem to matter. We never spend even a small fraction of our budgets. The interests I've targeted (Mysteries, Thrillers, Suspense) have only a little to do with the book Firebird. But that shouldn't impact number of impressions. All I care about is impressions. I'll worry about clicks and click through rate (CTR) later.

Results after 17 days at $0.10 ACPC

Days	Impressions	Sales	ACoS
17	113,464	8	218.07%

$0.10 Bid per click is killing me. I spent $53.80 and made $24.67. Thus my ACoS is so high. I'm going to edit my bid to $0.05.

Results after 9 days from changing my bid to $0.05

Days	Impressions	Sales	ACoS
9	137,082	7	155.26%

This is not a clean result because it's connected to my $0.10 CPC bid. The $0.05 campaign was better but it fizzled out.

Amazon just added an action called "Copy." It allows you to copy past ads. Firebird's best campaign was Firebird 3. I will try the copy function but add her new heading and text. The first time I tried I got an error message. I just deleted the draft and tried again and called it Firebird 7. I'm hoping after resting for about 20 days (staying away from the same targeted interests) that this campaign will run as good as Firebird 3.

Campaign name	**Firebird 7**
Book	Firebird
Ad locations	Detail pages on Amazon.com
Targeting type	Interest-based
Targeted Interests	5 Interests selected
CPC bid	$0.05
Budget	$500.00

Duration	02/19/2016–03/20/2016
Pacing	Deliver my campaign as quickly as possible
Kindle book price	$2.99

After ten days we've had only 3 impressions. I don't know if it's because it's a repeat ad or if it is because it's simultaneous. But I will keep it going for a few more days. After 12 days (3/2/2016) still 3 impressions. After 20 days a total of 4 impressions. Time to cancel this ad. What does this mean? Re-running and ad doesn't seem to work. I either need to change my CPC bid or change my interests. But copying a successful ad that eventually fizzled out doesn't seem to revive it.

* * *

Good Morning Glory

8 Five Stars reviews

Headline: Jane Austin meets Dorothy Parker in 1926

Ad text: James West is handsome, rich, and unattainable. His housekeeper, Kit, should be off limits, but she's got more than the usual charms to recommend her.

Campaign name	**Good Morning Glory 1**
Book	Good Morning Glory
Ad locations	Detail pages on Amazon.com
Targeting type	Interest-based
Targeted Interests	3 Interests selected: Historical Romance, Under teen and young adult-Historical Fiction and Romance
CPC bid	$0.05
Budget	$500.00
Duration	12/23/2015–01/22/2016
Pacing	Deliver my campaign as quickly as possible
Kindle book price	$2.99

* * *

Results after 21 days

Impressions	546,489
Clicks	4,495
CTR	.823% (Click through rate)

Spend	$183.95
ACPC	$0.04 (Average cost per click)
Estimated orders	128
Estimated total sales	$388.16 128 books at $2.04 = $261.12

$261.12 made - $183.95 spent = $77.17 profit.

Shaunna's click through rate is great. The orders are 1 order for every 35 clicks. That's amazing! On Wheelz and Firebird our orders are about 1 for every 50 clicks.

Before I started any ads, I went on line to see how people liked Kindle Ad Campaigns. I found the following:

LindseyBuoker.com

Amazon Advertising Services for Indie, Authors, Yea or Nay?

Her blog and comments from others who had tried Kindle ads concluded basically that they are useless.

Andrew said on 03/03/15

> I tried this as well. After a month of gradually increasing my maximum payment per click, I ended with about 16000 impressions, 40 clicks, and a total of 1 sale. That one sale for a 3.99 book cost me 7.99. If I had been more patient and left my payment per click lower, I probably

wouldn't have lost as much money, but I also may not have seen even that single sale.

Honestly, the numbers just seem too small to bother with the service at this point, at least in my experience.

Christine Fairchild said on 09/04/2015

"Ads are never better than direct marketing channels, such as BookBub, ENT, etc. That's been true for 100 years. Advertising is for building brand/presence, not sales."

I don't know, $77 profit with 128 book orders sounds pretty good to me. And Shaunna has two books. Once those 128 people finish *Morning Glory* they will be looking for *Firebird*. She is building brand/presence and she is also making sales. She right now is an unknown author in the book world. And yet 128 people were willing to give her a try.

Shaunna is doing much better on her campaigns than I am. This should be encouraging to beginning fiction authors. Obviously if her books are not engaging they will not continue to be successful. But she is a good writer. She is working on her third book and plans to write many more. Kindle Ads are gold for her.

Campaign name	**Morning Glory 2**
Book	Good Morning Glory
Ad locations	Detail pages on Amazon.com
Targeting type	Product-based
Targeted products	3 Interests selected (same as Morning Glory 1)
CPC bid	$0.05
Budget	$500.00
Duration	01/18/2016–02/17/2016
Pacing	Delivery my campaign as quickly as possible
Kindle book price	$2.99

Headline: Jane Austen meets Dorothy Parker in 1926

Ad Text: James West is handsome, rich, and unattainable. His housekeeper, Kit, should be off limits, but she's got more than the usual charms to recommend her.

Morning Glory 2 campaign is exactly the same as Morning Glory 1. Morning Glory 1 fizzled out at 500,000. We stopped the campaign and tried the same ad as a new campaign.

Results after 20 days

Impressions	45,738
Clicks	367
CTR	.802% (Click through rate)
Spend	$14.72
ACPC	$0.04 (Average cost per click)
Estimated orders	9
Estimated total sales	$26.78
ACoS	54.97%

Morning Glory 2 was not nearly as successful as Morning Glory 1 (which had half a million impressions in 21 days). And yet it is an okay campaign. We will not cancel this campaign yet.

Results after 30 days

Impressions	400,522
Clicks	3,365
CTR	.84% (Click through rate)
Spend	$135.52
ACPC	$0.04 (Average cost per click)

Estimated orders	95
Estimated total sales	$283.93
ACoS	47.73%

Morning Glory 2 took off the last 10 days. Shaunna made $148.41 and 95 people are reading her book from this campaign.

The reason I began this book talking about due diligence is I figured I could show that Kindle Ad Campaigns don't work. I could save people a lot of money and time if I could prove they weren't worth the effort. Everything I read about Kindle campaigns was negative. They were wrong. And by the way she made $381.27 in royalties for both books off the KENP (Kindle borrowing) program for the month of January.

I'm going to try re-running the campaign. The advantage is you don't have to re-submit for a new campaign. To re-run a campaign all you have to do is edit the end date. I changed it from 2/17/2016 to 3/17/2016. We'll call it Morning Glory 3 and see how it performs.

Campaign name	**Morning Glory 3**
Book	Good Morning Glory
Ad locations	Detail pages on Amazon.com
Targeting type	Product-based

Targeted products	3 Interests selected (same as Morning Glory 1 and 2)
CPC bid	$0.05
Budget	$500.00
Duration	02/16/2016–03/17/2016
Pacing	Deliver my campaign as quickly as possible
Kindle book price	$2.99

Results after 15 days

Impressions 115,511

Sales: Lost that data sorry. But impressions are respectable.

Morning Glory 3 has run its course. I will cancel it.

Results for December, January and February

Wheelz
Units sold: 81
KENP pages: 9,402
Spent: $179.72
Royalties earned: $179.53

Firebird
Units sold:120
KENP pages: 41,870
Spent: $203.46
Royalties earned: $430.75

Morning Glory
Units sold: 293
KENP pages: 105,805
Spent: $385.32
Royalties earned: $1,057.03

In the three months Wheelz got 8 new reviews. About 100 people are reading my book which cost me a total of $0.19. But my books kept selling in March when my campaigns ran dry. So I probably made a couple bucks over all.

Shaunna got many more reviews. But she sent out requests for reviews so we don't know how many were from her campaigns. It think it is a conservative estimate to suggest she got at least 12 reviews on her two books. I got 8 and she sold three times more books than me.

We could end this book here. We have definitely shown that Kindle Ads can work. But Firebird 7 is disconcerting. It was a copy of Firebird 3 which was a successful campaign and yet Firebird 7 only got 4 impressions. Does Amazon limit exposure? I will cancel all our ads and start again. I need to show if we can get other successful ads by targeting new interests or products categories or upping the bids.

Campaign name	Wheelz 24
Book	Wheelz
Ad locations	Detail pages on Amazon.com
Targeting type	Interest-based
Targeted Interests	Education and Teaching; Teaching resources
CPC bid	$0.05
Budget	$500.00
Duration	03/10/2016–04/09/2016
Pacing	Deliver my campaign as quickly as possible
Kindle book price	$2.99

Results: After 30 days Wheelz 24 got 447 impressions and 1 click. I do not understand the dismal results.

Campaign name	Firebird 8
Book	Firebird
Ad locations	Detail pages on Amazon.com
Targeting type	Product-based
Targeted products	8 Random books under "Romance"
CPC bid	$0.05
Budget	$500.00
Duration	03/10/2016–04/09/2016
Pacing	Deliver my campaign as quickly as possible
Kindle book price	$2.99

March 26, 2016, Sixteen days into this campaign with 0 impressions. I'm going to cancel it and try a new campaign. I think only targeting 8 books was a mistake.

Campaign name	Firebird 9
Book	Firebird
Ad locations	Detail pages on Amazon.com

Targeting type	Interest-based
Targeted Interests	Romance: Romance suspense and fantasy
CPC bid	$0.05
Budget	$500.00
Duration	03/26/2016–04/25/2016
Pacing	Deliver my campaign as quickly as possible
Kindle book price	$2.99

Results: After 30 days Firebird 9 got 57 impressions and no clicks. I know it's stupid but I need to see what's going on. I will bid $0.25 per click to see if we can generate any impressions.

Campaign name	**Firebird 10**
Book	Firebird
Ad locations	Detail pages on Amazon.com
Targeting type	Interest-based
Targeted Interests	Romance: Contemporary, Inspirational, Romantic Comedy

CPC bid	$0.25
Budget	$350.00
Duration	04/16/2016–04/30/2016
Pacing	Deliver my campaign as quickly as possible
Kindle book price	$2.99

Results after 16 days

Impressions	94,7347
Clicks	585
CTR	.62% (Click through rate)
Spend	$146.25
ACPC	$0.25 (Average cost per click)
Estimated orders	7
Estimated total sale	$20.93
ACoS	698.76%

That ACoS is pathetic. I cannot see any value in bidding $0.25 per click. We lost $120.00 to sell seven books. 94,737 impressions is respectable but not worth the cost.

I want to try a Morning Glory campaign targeting several interests.

Campaign name	Morning Glory 4
Book	Good Morning Glory
Ad locations	Detail pages on Amazon.com
Targeting type	Interest-based
Targeted Interests	8 interest selected
CPC bid	$0.05
Budget	$500.00
Duration	03/10/2016–04/09/2016
Pacing	Deliver my campaign as quickly as possible
Kindle book price	$2.99

Using a lot categories may be a mistake. It seems like Amazon keeps track of categories you use. We could use them all up. We'll see.

Results: After 30 days Morning Glory 4 got 48 impressions.

It seems like Amazon lets a book only get so much exposure. To test that I need to introduce a new book into our study. Lisa Swinton, a friend of mine, self-published a few books. She allowed me to run a campaign on one of her books titled Fallen Angel. It is a romantic fiction.

Campaign name	Fallen Angel 1
Book	Fallen Angel
Ad locations	Detail pages on Amazon.com
Targeting type	Interest-based
Targeted Interests	Romance
CPC bid	$0.05
Budget	$500.00
Duration	04/06/2016–05/06/2016
Pacing	Deliver my campaign as quickly as possible
Kindle book price	$2.99

Results after 30 days

Impression	400
Clicks	1
CTR	.27% (Click through rate)

Spend	$0.02
ACPC	$0.02 (Average cost per click)
Estimated orders	0
Estimated total sales	$0.00
ACoS	47.73%

To be honest I have no clue what's going on. Shaunna got about a half a million with the same bid and same targeted interests. We upped the bid for Morning Glory to see if that helps.

Campaign name	**Morning Glory 5**
Book	Morning Glory
Ad locations	Detail pages on Amazon.com
Targeting type	Interest-based
Targeted Interests	Historical Romance and a few others
CPC bid	$0.15
Budget	$500.00
Duration	04/16/2016–04/30/2016

Pacing	Deliver my campaign as quickly as possible
Kindle book price	$2.99

Results after 16 days

Impressions	158,031
Clicks	1,061
CTR	.67% (Click through rate)
Spend	$159.15
ACPC	$0.15 (Average cost per click)
Estimated orders	41
Estimated total sales	$123.63
ACoS	128.73%

The impressions are respectable. 41 sales is good. But we lost $35.52. I do not understand how bidding $0.10 less than Firebird 10 (bid $0.25 per click) got Morning Glory 63,297 more impressions. The interests targeted were not that different. Surely some of our loss will be made up with KENP. I think I would bid $0.15 again to market my books.

Sponsored Products

Kindle came out with "Sponsored Products" after I ran my 40 campaigns. But the principles are the same. You can bid a lot per day with no problem because they only charge per click. So I will bid $10 per day and probably raise that to $50 per day soon. I would gladly pay $500 a day at $0.05 per click. That would make money considering what we've learned on the ratio of purchases per number of clicks.

This will probably prove to be an even better way to run a campaign because it centers on ad words related to our books.

Conclusions:

1. Bidding $0.06 or over will cost us to sell our books.

2. It may be beneficial to take a loss to promote our books.

3. Kindle Edition Normalized Pages (KENP) can compensate for loosing campaigns.

4. Targeting interests is easier and probably as good, if not better, than targeting products.

5. Letting Amazon deliver our campaign as quickly as possible or smoothly ends up being about the same.

6. Simultaneous campaigns can bid against each other.

7. Simultaneous campaigns, even with different interests or products targeted, seem to slow down each other.

8. Sales + borrows seem to equal more sales.

9. $2.99 is the best break even (and maybe a little profit) point for a Kindle book.

10. $0.99 moves more books, but it will cost you to get your book out there.

11. $3.99 does not sell many books.

12. Targeting interests unrelated to our books seems to be as good as targeting related interests.

13. Ad campaigns slow down.

14. Re-running a successful ad can work.

15. Re-running an identical campaign most assuredly will not get the same results.

16. Kindle ads get our books out there.

17. A multiple book author can benefit much by running Kindle ads.

18. Running ads as a marketer may be wiser than as a book seller.

19. There are variables that we don't see like how many are bidding against us at a certain time. Therefore past success does not guarantee future success.

20. We can sell books and make money using Amazon Kindle Ad Campaigns.

I believe Amazon switches up their algorithms so that no one will figure out the perfect way to bid. If we did than everyone would bid that amount and that would ruin that combination. For example if we learned that $0.05 was the perfect bid amount and $500 was the right campaign amount it wouldn't take long before everyone would be bidding the same.

I wanted to find that perfect formula. I was willing to share it with my readers. I also wanted to prove Kindle ads don't work (like so many blogs profess) to save everyone a lot of time and money. But now and then they do work.

The bottom line is I am going to keep on promoting my book about my son. My bids will range between $0.05 and $0.15. I am willing to take a loss to get people talking about my book. And the nice thing is we only pay for clicks. Lisa and Shaunna are also continuing to run ad campaigns.

I talked about due diligence at the beginning of this book. I could have ended this book saying "Wow this really works. We made a best-seller. We made money." All of that is true. But then our ads fizzled out. That is also true. I needed to see if we could get impressions on the other side of worn out campaigns. We did, but it cost a bit.

I hope this helps. I hope you see something I missed which makes your ads more successful. If I have helped in any way would please leave me a kind review. A couple words is all I need. As an author you know why I ask this.

Thank you for joining me on this journey. I know what it's like to be passionate about producing a book. I am also well aware of an author's dream of success. And I know what it's like to be buried under a million other books. Maybe this will inspire you to keep campaigning. And hopefully it will help to get your book bobbing above the surface.

Thank you, Steven Fotheringham

About the Author

Steve Fotheringham has a Bachelor's Degree in Psychology from Weber State University, a Master's Degree in Marriage and Family Counseling and a Doctoral Degree in Educational Administration from The University of Arizona.

He is the author of the book *Wheelz.*

After running forty Kindle Ad Campaigns with four different books (three fictional and one biography) he can offer the results of his journey and some advice on running successful campaigns.

www.ingramcontent.com/pod-product-compliance
Lightning Source LLC
Chambersburg PA
CBHW060405190526
45169CB00002B/761